# MEAN GIRLS MEET
# JUSTICE

Dr. Lasonja Flowers-Ivory
with Aniyah Temple

COVER DESIGN AND ILLUSTRATIONS
by Jorge Contreras, Phobia Art
phobiaairbrushart@gmail.com

EDITING AND FORMATTING
Linda Stubblefield
www.affordablechristianediting.com

LOGO
CIR Design
www.cir-design.com

DISCLAIMER: While I chose to use the names of loved ones in this book, this is a work of fiction.

Printed in the United States of America

www.drsonjaivory.com

# DEDICATION

*To my very own Aniyah*

THIS BOOK IS dedicated to you, Aniyah, because you are the reason it has been written. When I picked you up from school on my last visit to California, you saw the cover of *Who Cares About Black Boys* and noticed two of your cousins were featured on the cover. I remember how your face lit up when you said, "GG, now we have to write a book for girls!" I laughed but you were serious, and you said, "Let's go to the library right now!" After we went to dinner, we went to the library and spent a few hours on this book. Now it's a reality!

Since the first day I learned of your existence, I have loved you. Your parents allowed me to be in the delivery room to watch the very moment of your arrival, and I will never forget that day. I didn't think I could love you anymore than I did on that day, but God has enlarged my heart; my love for you continues to grow. There's something about your smile, your laugh, your hugs and even the way you call my name that makes my heart smile. Sometimes, it's still hard to believe that my first son,has an eight-year-old daughter!

You're only eight, but we have shared some very special moments together. I remember when you were in kindergarten and told me that one of your classmates from a different religion brought you a pamphlet to school about their religion and wanted you to join them. We talked about Jesus that day, and God allowed me to be the tool to lead you to Christ. That's the best day ever.

Aniyah, you are a gift from God. My prayer is that you will get to know Jesus as your friend and become His.

# ACKNOWLEDGMENTS

Eric Ivory, thank you for your constant support. I really like being your wife.

Alonzo Temple and Princeton Temple, I look forward to building memories and growing with you both.

Derrick Temple, Jr. (Aniyah's dad), thank you for sharing your scheduled time with Aniyah with me. I love the relationship we have; I wouldn't trade it for anything.

Velexia Droughn (Aniyah's mom), thank you for the relationship that we have and encouraging the relationship I have with Aniyah with total access to her life.

Marie Flowers, my mother, I love you for giving me your best.

My family and friends, thank you for seeing and supporting me as an author. I love you all.

Linda Stubblefield, thanks for being the editor who also inspires!

Thank you to Jorge Contreras of Phobia Art for exceeding my dreams for the art.

Thank you to parents and educators who help to make schools safe for children everyday.

Special recognition to Jacqueline Byrd, Dr. Wanda Bolton-Davis, and Cheryl Wesley—my Texas Sisterhood. Your friendship has enriched my life. Let's keep growing together.

My love and appreciation to two of my newest sisters in Christ, Robin Lage and Elizabeth Strickland.

Thank you to my newly drafted business manager, John Lage.

A very special recognition for my childhood friend, Sharon Fisher.

# TABLE OF CONTENTS

# PROLOGUE

MY NAME IS Justice Candor, and I am an only child. I love school, but my last school year at Bivin Elementary School was tough. My parents were so unhappy together, they finally divorced. For my sake, they decided to continue to parent me together. I'm glad because I love both my mom and my dad. We plan to have dinner together once a week. Most of the time, Daddy comes to our house. Sometimes we meet at a restaurant. I love these times when we are all together.

When the school year finished, my family and I moved away from my friends and my cousins. I had been looking forward to being promoted to fourth grade so I could learn from my favorite teacher, and now I have to transfer to a new school. I feel so sad about all these changes. My life feels so different. I remember all the good times at my old school. I had a lot of friends, and I looked forward to going to school every day.

My cousins Nylia, Brittny, and Kiandrea also attended my school. Seeing them every day was fun. Sometimes our moms allowed us to go home with each other after school. We did our homework together, and then we played until dinner. How I loved those times with my cousins.

I am so thankful for those memories…

# CHAPTER ONE

# QUESTIONS

I LOVED MY FORMER school. I liked my friends and enjoyed being with them—even though we were all different. Some of my friends were tall; some were short. Some of them had long hair, some had short hair, some had straight hair, some had curly hair, and some wore braids. Our differences didn't matter to us. We knew that different was good, and we were all friends.

My cousins, Nylia, Brittny, and Kiandrea, are really smart. They wear their hair *natural.* They don't have perms or use chemicals in their hair. I like to wear my hair in ponytails, but when it is not in braids, I enjoy other styles for a change.

Some of the girls would ask us questions about our hair like, "How do you get your hair like that?" "Can I touch your hair?"

At first, their questions seemed weird. Sometimes my cousins and I didn't know what or how to feel or even how to answer their questions. But I do know our friends were being sincere.

One day, my dad picked up my cousins and me from school and heard us talking about the questions our friends had asked. He turned down the music he had been listening to and asked, "Girls, what do you do when you want information?"

We just looked at each other because we had no idea what he was talking about. Then I remembered that my dad hears everything. I said, "Daddy, it's weird to ask people to touch their hair, right? I have never asked other girls questions about their hair."

Dad asked again, "Girls, what do you do when you want information?"

My cousins and I looked at each and giggled.

He stared at us through the rearview mirror until he stopped at a traffic light. Then he turned around to face us. I was glad to see he didn't look angry. I knew he was waiting for an answer from me.

I looked at my cousins, and they looked at me. Finally, we all said together, "Well, we ask questions."

"Well, girls, it looks to me like you have the

answers to the questions that your friends need answered. What you have experienced is what I call a *teachable moment.*"

~

We spent the rest of the ride being quiet and looking out the window. Once Dad pulled into the driveway, we ran inside the house, dropped our backpacks, and headed to the backyard. I could tell that my cousins weren't thinking about playing like usual. We were all thinking about what my daddy had said.

"I have never heard my dad talk about *teachable moments,*" I said hesitantly.

"Justice, how can we have teachable moments if they don't ask us any more questions?" Brittny asked.

"Yeah, maybe they will forget all about our hair," Kiandrea added.

"Justice, you're being awfully quiet. What do you think?" Nylia questioned.

I looked up to the sky because that's what I

do when I am not sure how to say something or what to say. My cousins know me so well. They ran over to where I was looking at the sky and grabbed my hands. "Come on, Justice. Just spit it out! Go ahead and say it!"

"You know we hear these same questions almost every day. They just have to work up the courage to ask us. So, we should plan how to answer their questions about our hair, and like my dad said, make it a teachable moment!"

My cousins agreed to my proposal, and the planning began that day.

# CHAPTER TWO

# TEACHABLE MOMENTS

O N ANOTHER DAY during the lunch hour, the same questions about our hair began again. Curious asked, "So, Justice, how long does it take you to wash your hair every morning? You must take really long showers to get out all the shampoo, huh? Do you brush it before you blow it dry? I saw a video on social media once, and I thought the steps were confusing."

Nylia must have forgotten our teachable-moment plan. Before I knew it, she started asking Curious her own questions. "Why in the world would we wash our hair every day?"

A few of the girls started to laugh at her question. I had the feeling they were laughing *at* us and not *with* us. I know my cousin disliked their laughter. She felt they were making fun of her for asking the question. I knew she wasn't being disrespectful.

But with a serious expression on her face, Curious responded, "Nylia, my mother says that I have to wash my hair every day so it's clean and won't smell. Don't you care if your hair is clean?"

Before Nylia could answer, Kiandrea explained, "Most people know that Black girls' hair doesn't need to be washed every day to be clean. Our hair is dry and washing it every day would only make it even more dry. Daily washing would not be good for our hair."

Brittny added, "Plus, because we don't wash it every day, we spend a lot of time and money on our hairstyles. We wouldn't want to wash it every day."

Now, my cousins and I are laughing as we share about our personal haircare.

Nylia chimed back in, "Wait, Curious, you really do wash your hair every day? Does that schedule change when you get older? So, even when your moms go to the salon and pay to get their hair done, they wash it the next day? Wow! That sure seems like a waste of money."

Curious, her friends, and my cousins all started giggling at Nylia's questions.

I laughed too, but I was also thinking about our teachable-moment plan.

"So, Curious, does that washing-your-hair-everyday thing ever change for people with hair like yours?"

Curious responded, "Not until you get older. I guess the hair must change."

We all laughed again. I realized that this lunchtime had been full of teachable moments for all of us!

# CHAPTER THREE

# DIFFERENT IS GOOD

OUR FAVORITE TEACHER, Miss Price, stopped by our table to see why we were all laughing and having such a good time. When we replayed our conversation about hair, she said, "I'm so proud of you girls for being considerate enough to ask questions. The care of hair can be a sensitive topic, and you are being respectful enough of each other's feelings to ask questions.

"Be careful when discussing differences because people can get their feelings hurt easily. Always remember that different is good. This world is better because we are not all the same. I want you all to know that your topic involves the *texture* of hair—not necessarily Black hair or White hair or Brown hair. There are many different textures of hair. Some textures are oily, and therefore, must be washed regularly. Some are dry, and consequently need more oil. Some are a mixture of textures and require a combination of care."

Miss Price looked around the table at all of us and smiled. "Girls, now that you understand that different is good, I challenge you to share it every time you have an opportunity. An English statesman named Sir Francis Bacon said, 'Knowledge is power,' and knowledge helps us understand each other better. Always remember, different is good."

We returned from lunch feeling smart! I couldn't wait to go home after school and Facetime my grandmother! I call her GG. She loves talking about stuff like this. I surely had so much to share with her about today.

# CHAPTER FOUR

# ROLE MODELS

O N THE WAY to school the next day, I told my daddy what had happened at lunchtime. He smiled and told me that my teacher had called to ask if I could present that conversation to the class as a model of how to discuss differences. Daddy said, "Justice, I thought her suggestion was a particularly good idea. I think you and your cousins should do as the teacher requested for the class."

"Okay, Daddy," I agreed, "as long as my cousins will join me in the discussion."

At first, I was afraid that I would be the only one to talk in front of the class. I was so relieved when Brittny, Nylia, and Kiandrea all said yes! We were nervous as we thought about talking in front of our classmates. We just didn't know how they would take what we said.

As we shared, we could tell the class was really listening to us. They seemed to care about what we were saying. They even asked more questions!

When one person tried to make a joke out of our presentation, Miss Price interrupted her and kindly said, "These young ladies have courage to stand up in front of their classmates to discuss a difficult topic. Many adults do not have the courage to have these kinds of conversations. These girls are leaders, and I am proud of them."

The person became quiet.

We all smiled at Miss Price's kind words. *I am proud to be a leader,* I thought. I looked at my cousins, and I could tell they were also happy that we had agreed to talk to our class about differences. *They are leaders too!*

I didn't know it at the time, but our principal, Dr. Bolton, had slipped into the back of the room to listen. She clapped loudly for us at the end. When everyone turned to see who was clapping, she said, "Miss Price, may I please speak to your class?"

Miss Price replied, "Of course, Dr. Bolton. I know the class would love to hear your thoughts."

"Thank you, Miss Price. First, I want to thank these brave girls for being respectful of each other's differences. After hearing them,

I think more of our students should hear this conversation."

My cousins and I just eyed each other with puzzled looks.

"I would like for all of you to present this conversation again in front of all of the third-grade classes in the auditorium. You are the kind of role models I want the other students to know."

Before I knew it, I exclaimed, "Role models? We were only talking about hair!"

Dr. Bolton responded, "No, Justice, it's more than hair. I agree that hair is the subject, but hair is intricately connected to identity for some people. I believe your conversation teaches many lessons that need to be learned. I will be calling your parents tonight to give them more information to share with you about what I would like. I hope you all will agree to do this presentation again."

When Principal Bolton left, the entire class

clapped for us! *Now we have to do it,* I groaned to myself.

～

That night Dr. Bolton called my parents and my cousins' parents for permission from them. She also explained to them how to coach us on some specifics. That night Dad stayed after we had dinner together. He and Mom both helped me prepare for a second presentation.

The next day we again presented our conversation about differences. After the assembly concluded, everybody around seemed to be discussing our talk. People now knew our names, and we made many new friends. In two days, my cousins and I had become school stars—without even trying!

*This is so the perfect school!*

# CHAPTER FIVE

# HURTING PEOPLE WOUND PEOPLE

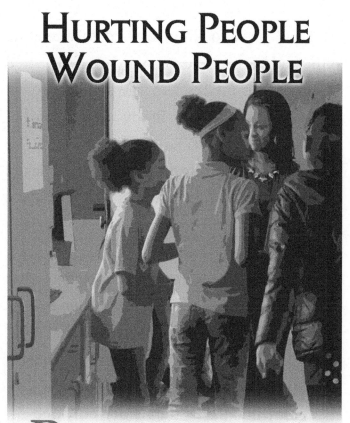

BECAUSE MY PARENTS divorced at the end of the school year, my mom and I now live in a new home in a new-to-me neighborhood. I will soon be attending a new school—Douglas Elementary School. I now have a new life—one I really did not want.

I had been looking forward to attending fifth grade at my old school. I really wanted Dr. Brody for my teacher. The truth is, everyone wanted to have Dr. Brody as a teacher because she was nice, smart, and very pretty. She had been a nurse before she became a teacher. Sometimes she let her students wear her white lab coat. She even let the students wear her stethoscope draped around their neck!

Being a nurse someday sounds nice, but right now, I am not sure that's what God wants me to do with my life. I try not to think about going to a new school. When I think about no Dr. Brody at my new school, I feel so sad.

On my first day at the school, only one girl talked to me. Her name was Kimberly, and I think she only talked to me because the teacher told her to show me around. The next day, though, I was surprised to see Kimberly waiting for me at the front of the school with some of her other friends. "Justice, why don't you come to the cafeteria and sit with us when the bell rings?"

I was so excited to be included! Of course, I said yes.

As I looked around me, I saw many other kids there and realized this school was much bigger than my former school. Since I did not know the girls, I listened to their conversations, staying quiet the entire time.

The room was so noisy, I wanted the bell to ring so I could go to our classroom for some peace and quiet. When I'm in a hurry for something to happen, my mom always says, "Justice, a watched pot never boils." She had to explain this proverb to me so I could understand what she was saying. She said, "Time seems to move more slowly when you are waiting." Finally, the bell rang, and I could now go to a smaller space with less noise.

When I walked into my homeroom, my teacher called me by my name—even though

I was a new student. "Justice, my name is Mrs. Donnison. I'm so glad you will be a student in my class. Let me show you to where you'll be sitting in row five, seat two."

I smiled at her, glad that she had remembered my name and recognized me. I took my seat and put my school supplies in my desk. As I waited for the starting bell to ring, I began thinking about the changes in my life. *I miss my old school and my old life. My mom and my dad both seem angry all the time. Sometimes, I wish I could fix our family, but I don't know what I did to break it up. If I only knew. I would give anything for things to go back to the way they were. Maybe I should have kept my room clean. Maybe I should have done my chores better. Maybe I should have gone to bed on time... Maybe tomorrow will be better.*

⁓

Well, two weeks have passed slowly, and I have finally made some new friends. They are not like having my cousins, but they are nice, and I enjoy being with them.

One day in class, Mrs. Donnison asked us to raise our hands if we had ever learned something from someone who was different from us. My hand flew up immediately because I thought about our hair conversation that had made me famous in my last school. When Mrs. Donnison asked me to share my experience with the class, I was so excited. *Maybe this will be a repeat of what happened at my last school! Maybe everyone will want to be my friend, and I won't be so lonely anymore.*

I described how my cousins and I talked about differences in hair to our class. "My principal heard us tell about our experience, and she asked us to present it to the third-grade class."

When I finished, Mrs. Donnison praised me for what my cousins and I had done. I even noticed that some of my classmates were smiling.

*This is going to be a great day! A great school!* I thought excitedly.

~

On the way to lunch, I stopped in the restroom. Suddenly I heard some voices giggling by the stall door. When I tried to open the door, I couldn't. They laughed at my efforts.

I recognized the voices, so I said, "Hey! That's real funny. You had your joke. Please step away from the door now. I would like to go to the cafeteria."

But nobody moved away from the door. Then Tanesha hatefully taunted, "You think you are smarter than us because you were a star at your last school."

"No way, Tanesha! I was only telling a story. Now let me out. Please let me out."

Tanesha and her friends kept giggling and blocking the door.

Then Nakia mocked me, repeating in a sing-song voice, "No way, Tanesha! I was only telling a story. Now let me out! Please let me out! Please let me out!"

I felt tears coming to my eyes, so I tried to laugh and pretend that what they were doing was all a joke.

"Very funny! This was a good one, but I'm getting hungry now. Please let me out so I can go to lunch."

Nakayla spitefully said, "Oh, but you don't have a lunch!"

When I heard my lunch pail being opened, I began to push harder on the stall door. No matter how hard I pushed, I couldn't get the door open.

"Wow! Justice has cookies and juice and a sandwich in her lunch," another voice I didn't recognize chimed in.

*How does she know my name?*

When all the girls rushed over to see my lunch, I was finally able to open the door. I couldn't believe what I was seeing. Two of them were my classmates! I didn't know the other two, but they were so rude and unkind. I was so happy to get out of the stall I didn't even try to get my lunch pail. I sat in the cafeteria alone and started to cry. Nobody seemed to notice that I was crying and that I didn't have a lunch.

When I returned to the classroom, Tanesha and Nakayla were looking at me, pointing, and laughing. Tanesha walked by my desk and whispered, "You better *not* tell the teacher."

Anytime Mrs. Donnison came near my desk, I could tell they were watching me to see if I would tell on them. I didn't. I even stayed after school to help my teacher just to avoid them on the school bus.

"Justice, you're being noticeably quiet. Is everything all right?" she asked.

"Mrs. Donnison, something happened in the girls' restroom today." I told her about being held in the stall and their taking my lunch.

"Justice, I am so sorry that these girls acted

that way and hurt you the way they did. My best advice is for you to ignore them."

"Okay, Mrs. Donnison, I will try. I know it will be hard though. They are so mean."

"Yes, Justice, I understand that they were very unkind. If they try to hurt you again, just remember that hurt or wounded people wound people. They wouldn't try to hurt others if they weren't already hurting."

⁓

I thought about Mrs. Donnison's words all the way home. *Hurt or wounded people wound people. I never want to be the kind of person who hurts others.*

When I got home, I saw Dad's car in the driveway. *He's here for dinner,* I thought. *I hope he doesn't notice I don't have my lunch pail.* When I walked in the house, Dad greeted me happily. "Hi, Sweetie! I've missed you. Justice, where's your lunch pail? Did you forget to bring it home?"

"Dad, this new school is so big, I lost it. I'm sorry, Dad. I know you had to pay for it. I'll check lost and found tomorrow. Hopefully, I will be able to find it there."

I did not know what else to do, so I lied to him. I hated not telling my dad the truth, but if I did, he would tell my mom. They both would come to the school, and I just know that would make everything worse.

# CHAPTER SIX

# BULLY

THE NEXT DAY, I was sitting in class working on my classwork when Tanesha walked by my desk and cut my hair with scissors she had hidden in her pocket. At first, I didn't know what she had done, but my classmates seated around me started looking at me, pointing, and laughing. Then Nakayla came to my desk and leaned down to pick up something she saw lying on the floor. She placed it on my desk and continued to walk nonchalantly along the aisle.

*It's my braid!* I was so shocked, I started crying and put my head down on my desk. *I can't believe this is happening to me. What did I ever do to them?*

I knew I had to tell Mrs. Donnison—no matter what they did to me. I stood and walked to the teacher's desk and told her what had just happened.

She stood. "Nakayla and Tanesha, leave now and go to the principal's office," she ordered in a voice I had never heard her use before.

Mrs. Donnison gave me a tissue so I could dry my eyes and took my hand. "Justice, what those girls did to you was cruel. I'm so sorry. Remember what I told you? Hurting people hurt people. Please try to ignore them."

I nodded. I was so glad they were out of the classroom. At least now I felt safer.

One of my classmates named Adrienne walked over to me and said, "Justice, what Nakayla and Tanesha did was wrong. I'm glad you told the teacher."

Her kind words encouraged me, and I began to feel better.

But then another girl named Consuelo came to warn me about a possible situation. "Justice, Nakayla has two sisters who also go to this school. Tanesha is their cousin. If I were you, Justice, I would go back to my old school. You had better be careful."

*Oh no, now what is happening? I wish I never would have told my story about the hair at my old school. I so wish I could call my grandmother right now; she always knows what to do. Well, thankfully, they are meeting with the principal, and she will fix everything. I will remember that hurt and wounded people hurt people.*

*I will forgive them. I'll just accept their apology and move on.*

~

After school, two girls I recognized from the bathroom walked up to me and greeted me, "Hi, Justice."

I said, "Hello."

One of the two girls said, "Ny name is Nakia; I'm Nakayla's sister and Tanesha's cousin." She pointed to the girl with her and said, "This is Koquise—Nakayla's other sister and Tanesha's cousin too."

Before I could say anything, Nakia screamed, "Why did you get my sister and my cousin in trouble?"

Instead of answering, I turned and walked toward my bus as fast as I could. When I got to where I boarded the bus, I saw Tanesha and Nakayla waiting for me with angry looks.

Tanesha knocked my glasses off my face and stomped on them. She started to push me, but

Mrs. Evans, the bus driver stepped off the bus to see why people were gathered around laughing and pointing.

"Justice," she ordered, "Get on the bus." The three sisters and their cousin were all laughing and pointing at me as the bus drove off. I knew I needed to do something different. *Think Justice, think.*

~

I knew I needed to talk to my parents. I knew I was not wise enough to handle this problem alone. I needed their help. Before I walked through the door, I pulled my hair into a ponytail so Mom wouldn't see it had been cut until we talked. I knew my dad was coming for dinner that night, so I decided to wait until I could talk to both of them at the same time.

I quickly kissed my mom on the cheek. Before she had time to ask me about my day, I asked, "Mom, would it be okay for me to call my cousins and my grandmother?"

Thankfully, she didn't suspect anything. "Sure," she answered.

I ran to my room and closed the door.

When I told my cousins what was happening at school, they told me that new girls are bullied a lot. "Justice, if you don't stand up to them, they will never stop."

Then Kiandrea scared me with her next statement. "Justice, if you tell your parents or the teachers or the principal, they will call you a snitch. I'm just saying…"

Brittny chimed in and added, "That's true, Justice, but do it anyway! Remember, we are leaders."

"Nylia, aren't you going to say something?" I asked.

"Justice, you're gonna have to fight her."

"Fight her? Fight who? You know I don't get in fights."

Nylia responded, "You will have to fight whoever all the girls are following."

I just held the phone. I could not believe what my cousin Nylia had just said. I had never had a fight with anyone. I mean, sure, we used to put on boxing gloves with our boy cousins when my daddy trained them on the how-tos of boxing, and we had fun. But I knew what she was talking about was different than playing at boxing. We talked a while longer, and I hung up with my cousins.

Now I knew for sure I needed to talk to my grandmother. I can tell her anything. GG is always happy to see me and always happy to talk to me.

When I told GG everything my cousins had told me, she surprised me when she agreed with them. "Justice, your cousins told you right. Those bullies don't want you to tell anyone, but remember, nothing good grows in the dark. You cannot keep this bullying a secret.

"But GG, Nylia thinks I will have to fight the leader. Are you saying she is right too?"

Grandma responded, "That will depend on how the school and her parents respond. You are being bullied, Justice. Bullying is not only wrong, it's also against the law. "If you do have to fight, remember those times you would have fun boxing with your cousins? Remember, fighting someone is just like boxing with gloves."

"But, GG, their bullying me has only happened a few times. I don't want to fight anyone!" Then I comprehended what GG had said. "Is it really true that bullying is against the law? Wow, this is worse than I thought."

Grandma agreed with me. "Yes, Justice, this bullying is worse than you thought." She prayed for God to give me wisdom and courage to do right. I knew that meant the next step was talking to my parents and being truthful with them.

～

After dinner, I told my parents that I needed to have a serious talk with them. First, I took my hair out of the ponytail holder. My mom was calm when she saw my braid was missing, but my dad thought I had cut my own hair again. Mom knew something else was involved, but she waited for me to tell the whole story, so I told them everything. When I finished telling about the restroom, my stolen lunchbox, and my broken glasses, Mom and Daddy started asking more questions.

"Justice," Mom asked, "why did you wait to tell the teacher? We have always taught you to involve adults in these problems."

Daddy started asking questions too. "Why did you wait so long to tell us?"

"Daddy, I honestly thought it would just go away."

"Justice, honey, trouble doesn't just go away on its own. Even as a grade schooler, you must start getting used to making decisions to protect yourself."

"Justice, sweetie, I would like you to repeat

the entire story to both of us one more time," Mom encouraged.

After she heard the story for a second time, she reached in her purse for her cell phone to call the school. As she dialed the number, she said, "Justice, I am calling Principal Sanchez to ask for a meeting with the other girls and their parents."

When the principal answered Mom's call, she listened to the entire story about my being bullied. As for Mom's request to have a meeting with everyone involved, she explained that she would only be able to meet with the other families separately. Mom had put on the speaker, and I heard Dr. Sanchez say, "Mr. and Mrs. Candor, I appreciate your involvement in Justice's life, and I do want to meet with both of you and Justice tomorrow morning. I will look forward to meeting you at 8:00 a.m.," Dr. Sanchez ended the conversation.

❧

I didn't sleep very well that night. Even though I desperately wanted to, I knew that I could not go back to my old school or my old life. I needed to plan—kinda like the "teachable-moment" plan. I needed to be prepared for what was coming next.

# CHAPTER SEVEN

# MEETING WITH THE PRINCIPAL

THE NEXT MORNING, I really didn't want to go to school. Daddy and Mom both said that I needed help. "Justice, we need the help of Dr. Sanchez in caring for this matter of bullying. I know you are scared, and I know you don't want to cause trouble for those girls who are involved. However, sweetie, someone needs to speak up and stop this before it gets worse. We are going to school, and we are going to have that appointment." I knew there was no point in arguing.

The school secretary, Miss Jingles, invited us to wait in Dr. Sanchez's office as she made some final announcements to the students. "Justice, Dr. Sanchez has instructed me to ask you to write exactly what happened during these incidents. I need you to sign your account and date it. It's especially important we keep a record of these incidents," Miss Jingles concluded.

As we waited for Dr. Sanchez to finish the announcements, I completed the form that described what had happened in the bullying incidents. The whole time I wrote, I hoped Dr. Sanchez would talk only to my parents. When she came into the office, she closed the door and then sat down at her desk. Was I ever surprised when she started to question me!

"Justice, did you tell anyone that the girls wouldn't let you out of the bathroom stall?"

"They warned me not to tell, and I was scared at first. But I stayed after school, and Mrs. Donnison could tell something was wrong. She finally got me to tell her what happened."

"Did you tell anybody about them cutting your hair?"

I didn't answer out of fear. So many thoughts were running through my mind. *If I say I was afraid to tell Mrs. Donnison because I didn't want her to get in trouble, and she does get in trouble, she will be upset with me for telling about the bullying. I'm already having trouble with the students...if my teacher is upset at me too, that will be even worse!*

I still didn't answer when Dr. Sanchez repeated the question.

My dad interrupted my galloping thoughts and said softly, "Justice, you must tell the truth about everything. You are not in trouble."

"Yes, ma'am, I told her. That's why they were sent to the office."

Mom asked, "What did the teacher say to you, Justice?"

"Mrs. Donnison told me to ignore them. She said that hurt and wounded people wound people."

"Dr. Sanchez, how can my daughter simply ignore them? With all of the bullying that is happening around the nation and is on the news, *that* was a teacher's response? I believe that answer is totally unacceptable!" I could tell that Mom was not happy with my teacher.

"Mrs. Candor, I assure you that I will speak to Mrs. Donnison. Trust me, her response isn't my expectation at all in situations like this."

*Oh, no! Now Mrs. Donnison will surely hate me too,* I thought to myself.

I listened to Dr. Sanchez assure my parents that she would meet with the other girls and their parents. "Mr. and Mrs. Candor, I will put an end to this bullying," she promised. "I will be meeting with them at 9:00 this morning."

"Before we leave, Dr. Sanchez, I want to assure you that I believe you can handle this situation. I see no reason to involve the superintendent or the school board with this matter," Daddy reassured her.

Mom and Daddy walked part way with me to my classroom. As I returned to class, I hoped and prayed that Dr. Sanchez would keep her word about stopping the bullying.

∼

Dr. Sanchez greeted Tanesha and her mom, inviting them to take a seat in her office. They pushed past her without even saying hello. Before Dr. Sanchez could close her door, Tanesha's mom snorted, "I don't appreciate you calling and telling me to meet you down here with Tanesha. You done scared her to death thinking she in trouble! She a good girl. I also don't see why I have to miss work to come down here to the school about my daughter. This happened at school! When she's here, it's *your* job to care for the problems—not mine."

Dr. Sanchez ignored her comments. "Good morning, Mrs. Sparetherod. I want to thank you for coming in today. I know you and Tanesha have had some challenges over the past few years. Did you ever follow up with counseling as recommended?

"Nope, my baby don't need no counseling. She can be a little mean if she's mistreated, but my whole family is mean. She comes by meanness honest, but she don't need no counselor for that."

"You do know why we are here, correct?"

"Yeah, I hear some little girl ran home and got her parents involved in kids' stuff."

"No, ma'am!" Dr. Sanchez firmly replied. "This situation is far more serious than *kids' stuff*, as you put it. Do you realize that your daughter hid scissors to bring them to school to cut off that girl's hair? She broke a school rule to even carry a pointed instrument. Mrs. Sparetherod, we absolutely take bullying seriously at this school, and it's my job to make sure that school is a safe place for everyone who attends."

"Bullying? You accusin' my girl of bullying? Y'all act like this is something new. Bullying been going on for a long time. I was a bully in school, and I never went to the principal's office. I turned out just fine. The way I see it, either you be the bully or somebody gonna bully you. My baby ain't gonna be the one bullied! You can believe that."

"Mrs. Sparetherod, Tanesha will not be successful at our school if she continues to follow that rule. There will be consequences for her bullying actions."

"Kids will be kids! It ain't like she not be passing her classes. Where are the papers I need to sign? Tanesha need to get back in class, and I gotta get back to work."

"Tanesha will not be attending school today. She will be suspended for two more days. We will not tolerate this behavior on our campus."

"Oh, okay, then we will take it off campus. What do I need to sign?"

Dr. Sanchez looked at Tanesha. "Your behavior was wrong, Tanesha. You may not treat other students at this school in this manner. There is a law against bullying, and we will take this matter seriously."

Ms. Sparetherod interrupted, "A law? Don't you talk to my baby like that! She ain't no criminal! Don't you try to scare her like that! I already told you, she just a kid doing kid stuff. That girl just need to put on her big-girl panties and grow up!"

"Mrs. Sparetherod, if Tanesha returns with this same attitude of bullying, she will be moved to an alternative school. If she was the least bit scared about this meeting with me, maybe she needs to consider how she scared a girl with her bullying. Now, before you leave, Tanesha needs to write an account of these incidents and fill out this form. She needs to tell her part in the bullying, sign it, and date it. Here is some paper for her to write out her report."

"I don't have no time for this!"

Dr. Sanchez was shocked as Tanesha's mom tossed the paper back on the desk, grabbed Tanesha's hand, and pushed her way out of the office, slamming the door.

*I hope the next appointment goes better than this one.* She shook her head in dismay. *Someone must win the heart of that child if she has a chance for a good life. With a mom like that teaching her how to live...I don't know. I just don't know.* She sighed deeply.

∼

At 10:00 Dr. Sanchez greeted Nakia, Nakayla, Koquise, and their mom. "Please have a seat in my office," she said. "I will be right with you. I must take an unexpected call. Miss Jingles will bring some paperwork for each of the girls to fill out. According to the law, we must keep records of these unfortunate matters."

"Dr. Sanchez, please take your time. We are happy to wait for you."

Miss Jingles brought the papers and said, "Girls, I need you each to write exactly what happened during these incidents. Include your part in the bullying incident. Then you will each need to sign your account and date it."

As they waited for Dr. Sanchez to finish her call, the girls completed the form, describing their part in the bullying incidents.

When Dr. Sanchez returned to her office, she closed the door, took her seat, and apologized for making them wait. "Mrs. Balance, thank you for understanding that I had to take a call. Do you understand that we are having this meeting because your daughters and their cousin were involved in a bullying situation?"

"Yes, Dr. Sanchez, I do. I have spoken with

each one of them and explained how I was bullied in school and how the bullying caused me to hate school. I told my girls that I wasn't as brave as Justice. I didn't speak up, and the bullying went on for years."

"Girls, how does it make you feel to know that your mom was bullied like you were bullying Justice?"

"I feel bad so bad for Mom," Nakia spoke up. "I never thought about it like that. Listening to my mom talk about all the mean things that girls did to her upset me. Then she showed me how I was doing the same thing to Justice." Nakia started to cry.

"Nakayla, what do you have to say about what you did to Justice?"

Nakayla was already crying and could barely speak. "I was only following what Tanesha said to do because she said it would be fun."

Before Dr. Sanchez could comment, Mrs. Balance interrupted, "Don't you dare blame

Tanesha, Nakayla! You have a brain of your own. You made the decision to join in, you picked up the hair, and you set it on her desk. You also texted your older sisters and got them involved in youir bullying by threatening Justice at the bus stop!"

"Mom, I told you I'm sorry! I didn't think anyone's feelings were going to be hurt. I didn't think it was gonna go this far."

"That's the problem, Nakayla. You didn't *think* at all. You only thought about yourself and looking good to a bully. I didn't raise you to hurt other people or make fun of other people. Is it funny when people tease you about being smart, and they call you a *nerd?*"

"No, ma'am."

"Then why would you do the very same thing to someone else?"

"I don't know, Mom, but I promise it won't happen again."

"Nakayla, it had better not!"

"Koquise," Dr. Sanchez said. "It's your turn."

"Dr. Sanchez, I don't want to make anybody ever feel like my mom felt in school. I didn't even think what we did was bullying, but after talking to my mom, I do now. But…"

"But what, Koquise?"

"Oh, never mind."

"Go ahead, Koquise, I want to hear what you are thinking. My office is a safe place to talk. I will listen to what you have to say."

"Well, bullies *always* get away with bullying. This was my first time ever, and it doesn't seem fair that I got caught. Why did I get caught? Why am I the one in trouble when everyone does it?"

"First of all, Koquise, you are not the only one in trouble," Dr. Sanchez reminded her. "And I can tell you why you got caught. In fact, I'm glad you brought that up, Koquise, because you are right. Most of the time, the person being bullied doesn't tell anyone, and no one gets caught. But that response is absolutely wrong. Nothing good grows in the dark. When people speak up, a bully is exposed, and appropriate actions can be taken. When my children were growing up, I hoped they would get caught any time they did wrong."

"Really?" a shocked Koquise asked. "But why?"

"Because I wanted them to learn early in life there were consequences for doing wrong. Today, you are learning there are consequences for bullying Justice Candor."

"But, Dr. Sanchez, sometimes kids speak up and nothing happens and then we be like, 'that's why we don't tell,'" Nakia added.

"You're right too, Nakia. But remember this, everybody has a boss, and if a teacher doesn't do anything about your problem, tell your parents. Then you tell the principal, and if the principal doesn't do anything about the matter, there's the superintendent, who is the boss of the principal. If the superintendent doesn't get involved, then you and your parents can contact the school board. As you can see, following the chain of command may not be simple and you may have to tell more than one person, but the end result will be worth the effort. You will not only make your life better but also the lives of other students who may not have the courage to tell," Dr. Sanchez explained. "Do you understand?"

The girls chorused their answer: "Yes, ma'am!"

"Dr. Sanchez," Mrs. Balance said, "Thank you for seeing my girls and me this morning. I'm so glad we talked about this matter. I assure you that my daughters will not be following a bully while they live under my roof. If they step out of line, please call me. I want you to know that we will be reaching out to Justice's mom. Rest assured that all three of my girls will be apologizing to Justice in person."

"Thank you, Mrs. Balance, we need more parents in our school like you. Thank you, girls, for filling out the forms I needed."

"Thank you, Dr. Sanchez. We promise never to bully anyone again."

As Dr. Sanchez watched the Balance family leave her office, she breathed a big sigh of relief. *What a delight that mother is,* she thought. *She has won the hearts of those girls. If only more mothers cared like she does.*

# CHAPTER EIGHT

# NOT IN MY SCHOOL

THE NEXT FEW days were a little crazy at school for me. First, Dr. Sanchez called me into her office and told me about meeting with the girls who had been so mean to me. She didn't tell me everything that was said, but I could tell that she had a serious meeting with them all. "Justice, I wanted you to know that I followed through on my promise to stop the bullying."

That meeting with my principal made me feel good until Tanesha's friends kept telling me that she wanted to fight me now because I got her suspended from school.

I kept repeating what my mom had told me to say. "I don't want to hear anything that somebody else said. As far as I'm concerned, it's over." If I said it once that day, I know I said it fifty times. *Well, it sure felt like fifty times.*

I finally gathered the courage to talk to my teacher. "Mrs. Donnison, may I stay after school to help you?"

She smiled as she replied, "Yes."

"Mrs. Donnison, I'm sorry if I got you in trouble with the principal. I didn't mean to."

"Oh, Justice," she said. "I don't want you to worry. I didn't get into trouble, but I did have a good reminder not to take those matters lightly.

What happened to you was important, and you should feel safe in my class. You are my responsibility, and I want you to feel safe. I failed to do my best. Thank you for speaking up; you're brave."

I sure didn't feel brave, but I was so happy inside.

~

It was a beautiful day to walk home. My friend Princeton was still at school, so we walked together. He knew all about what had been happening in school.

"Justice, I think I should tell you I've been hearing some rumors about Tanesha."

"Princeton, I am going to focus on the good part of my day. I don't want to hear any rumors."

We laughed.

I decided to call my mom to tell her about my talk with Mrs. Donnison. While we were talking, my mom heard a car horn sound really loud. "Justice, what is that horn I hear?"

I turned around to look. "Mom! It's Tanesha and her mother! Mom, I'm scared."

"Justice, listen to me! Give your phone to Princeton. Tell him to record everything that happens."

"Okay, Mom." I handed my phone to Princeton, told him mom's message, and then turned around to see what Tanesha and her mom were doing.

While I was watching them, I could hear Princeton telling Mom where we were.

Tanesha's mom jumped out of the car, yelling, "Y'all can settle this right now; you not on school property. Tanesha, you already know what to do to a *snitch*."

When Tanesha walked up to me with her fists balled, I remembered what GG said, and before she could do anything to me, I socked her in the nose. I could tell she was shocked, and I hoped she would quit right then. But how could she when her mother was shouting at her to hit me! Then she began to punch at me, and I began to defend myself. Everything began happening so fast, all I remember is Tanesha's mom yanking my hair because I was on top of Tanesha, punching as if I had on boxing gloves. I knew I couldn't fight off both of them…

Then I heard police sirens, saw flashing lights and heard a police officer ordering, "Break it up!"

My mom arrived right then and asked Princeton for my phone. Luckily, he had videoed the whole encounter. When Mom showed it to the police, they arrested and handcuffed Tanesha's mom, putting her in the back seat of the police cruiser.

Mom and I waited there until someone came to pick up Tanesha. "Justice, I know that girl has been cruel to you, but I just don't feel right leaving her sitting on a curb waiting for someone to pick her up." Eventually, a family member came for Tanesha. Then we drove Princeton home.

After Princeton got out of the car, I exclaimed, "Mom, I've never been so glad to see you! I was so scared!"

~

Later that evening, we heard the doorbell ring. When I answered the door, I was shocked to see Nakia, Nakayla, Koquise, and their mom. Mom had come to the door also. "Hello, Mrs. Balance, I'm delighted to see you. Won't you please come in?"

We sat down in the living room, and Mrs. Balance told us about their meeting with Dr. Sanchez.

"Mrs. Candor, my daughters have something they want to say to Justice."

One by one, Nakayla, Nakia, and Koquise apologized to me. They even had tears in their eyes. When they asked me to forgive them, I was happy to.

"Justice, I want to say that I'm sorry too. I was bullied in school, and I never told—not in school and not until this happened to you. If I had told them how much bullying had hurt me in school, maybe my girls wouldn't have been part of bullying. I wish I had been brave like you. Will you forgive me for being quiet?"

"Oh, yes, Mrs. Balance. Of course, I forgive you. And I think you are brave for telling your story now."

Mom spoke up. "Well, I haven't started dinner quite yet. Why don't we order some pizza and use this time to start getting to know each other a little better?"

While Mom and Mrs. Balance were talking, the sisters asked me about my hair story from Bivin Elementary School. I shared what had happened with my cousins and me. The more we talked, the more we liked each other, and we decided to be friends. After hearing my story about teachable moments and differences, we also decided that we should have teachable moments about bullying.

When we shared our idea with our moms, they thought it was a great idea too!

"Justice," Mom said, "The first thing you girls should do is name your project."

After much discussion, we decided to name it "Not in My School!"

I cannot tell you how excited we were about our plan. As we said good night to our new friends, we had a plan in place.

~

After school every day, we worked on our speech and talked about what we wanted to say to our schoolmates. We had even come up with a slogan: *"Speak up, stand up, and grow up!"* We came up with several points to teach:

1) If you are unhappy or feel unsafe at school, something needs to change. **Speak up!**

2) If you see someone else being hurt, even by something as simple as name calling, **Speak up!**

3) When you are asked to join in making fun of someone else, **Stand up!** Think about the other person's feelings.

4) Nobody has the right to cause you pain. **Stand up!**

5) Bullies are immature and need to **Grow up!**

~

Our parents became involved in helping us with our plan to help our school. When we had fully developed our program, we decided the time had come to ask Dr. Sanchez if we could start a NIMS (**Not In My School**) Club.

We explained that in our club, we would be mentors for younger children and make posters to display about being kind and friendly and place them in the halls and some classrooms. Daddy even offered to buy t-shirts for everyone who joined the club. The plan included having assemblies and announcements that addressed bullying. An email address was created to report bullying to the counselor. After we presented our plan to Dr. Sanchez, she became the first person to join our club! After she joined, so did our parents!

~

I am happy to say that Tanesha never bothered me again. Dr. Sanchez moved her to another class of fifth graders. I would see her occasionally, but when she saw me, she would turn and go in another direction.

One day I realized I hadn't seen her in a long time. I was concerned, so I went to the office to ask about her. Because of the Privacy Act, all the office personnel could tell me was that she was no longer a student in our school. Then I heard that she had been sent to an alternative school because someone had reported her to the NIMS website for more bullying. I was sad for Tanesha. I hoped and prayed that someone would make a difference for Tanesha.

⁓

When my family went to visit my cousins, I was able to share the rest of the story. They were all so proud of me for standing up to the bully and telling my parents. I told GG that she was right; fighting was just like boxing with the gloves.

"Justice," she said, "Make sure that fighting is your very last resort because you are way too smart to think that's the only way to settle things."

*I am Justice, and I love school again.*

## THE END

# Other Books by
# LaSonja Ivory-Flowers

*"Encouragement to Worship While Wounded"*

## Dr. LaSonja Flowers-Ivory
*Foreword by Wanda Bolton-Davis*

I N THIS AMAZING testament of the personalized care and powerful love of God, LaSonja uses biblical texts and reflective questioning to assist readers with applying God's Word to their lives. As she documents the guiding, nurturing and protective hand of God, she triumphantly shares overcoming personal wounds, including the exposure of her former husband's diagnosis of HIV during their marriage. LaSonja often states that while her life was affected by his disease, God did not allow her to become infected with it. Hence, her choice for the title of this book.

Es Mi Historia
Su

"Un Aliento para Orar Mientras Está en Sufrimiento"

Dra. LaSonja Flowers-Ivory

Prefacio por Wanda Bolton-Davis

E N ESTE ASOMBROSO testamento del cuidado personalizado y el amor poderoso de Dios, La-Sonja utiliza textos bíblicos y cuestionamientos reflectivos para ayudar a los lectores a aplicar la Palabra de Dios a sus vidas. A medida que ella documenta la mano de Dios en su guía y protección, ella comparte de forma triunfante cómo pudo superar sus heridas personales, incluyendo estar expuesta a su exmarido, que había sido diagnosticado con VIH durante su matrimonio. LaSonja a menudo dice que, aunque su vida fue afectada por su enfermedad, Dios no la permitió infectarse con ella. De esto vie la elección del título para este libro.

Who Cares About Black Boys? "Moving from acknowledgment to advocacy" Dr. LaSonja Flowers-Ivory

**W**ho Cares About Black Boys? Schools are sending a message to and about African American males that does not convey they are valuable and intellectually capable of academic success.

In school, African Americans account for 32 percent of suspensions and 30 percent of all expulsions, yet they only represent 17 percent of the total school population.

In Texas, Black students represent 14.9 percent of the total preschool student enrollment, yet they account for 37.8 percent of students who received more than one out-of-school suspension.

This book offers hope and ideas for intervention.

Visit www.drsonjaivory.com